Cooking with Dried Beans

Sara Pitzer

CONTENTS

Introduction

Dried beans are good food. People have been eating them for at least 8,000 years. Today we have our regional favorites in every part of the country — Boston baked beans in New England, refried beans on the West Coast, chili in Texas, red beans and rice in Louisiana. We like beans because they taste good. And in this case, our tastes are nutritionally sound.

Cooked dried beans provide B vitamins: niacin, thiamin, riboflavin, B_6, and folic acid; minerals: calcium, phosphorus, magnesium, sulfur and potassium, plus traces of iron, manganese, and copper. Dried beans provide almost as much fiber per serving as bran and as much protein as 2 eggs or ⅛ pound of hamburger. While the protein in dried beans is incomplete, beans *in combination* with grains or dairy products provide all the essential amino acids of complete protein.

All this for only about 225 calories per cup of cooked beans.

For all this, most of us don't eat beans as often as we might because we tend to run out of ideas for cooking them once we've made bean soup, baked beans, and chili.

The recipes in this collection include regional favorites from all over the country, along with recipes that have become my family's favorites during the years I've experimented with good ways to cook beans. I've not included any of those bizarre recipes that tend to pop up when one is looking for the greatest number of ways possible to use a particular food. Recipes exist for bean cake with vanilla frosting and bean pie with meringue; some people undoubtedly would find them tasty and exotic, but appealing to the esoteric tastes among us is not my goal. I want to introduce you to the possibilities for using dried beans as good, basic, day-to-day standard fare, the kinds of dishes that are so good you want to prepare them again and again, and you rely on them when you want to feed people something you know they'll like.

Kinds of Beans

As you browse through the recipes, you may discover some calling for a bean you can't find where you live, because a few beans still seem to be popular only in certain parts of the country. In these cases, just substitute another similar bean. The following list and descriptions should help you.

White Beans

Baby Limas. These are the same baby limas you grow in your garden. You can dry your own if you grow extra. And you can buy them anywhere. They are one of the faster cooking beans.

Butter Beans. These are the large limas you grow in your garden. These, too, are a good variety to dry yourself. You can buy them everywhere in the country in grocery stores.

Great Northern Beans. Great northerns are a meaty, plump bean, somewhat larger than navy beans, commercially grown mostly in Idaho. They are good to use when you want the cooked bean to be quite soft or when you want to make a puree. You can buy them all across the country.

Marrow Beans. Marrows look something like a fat baby lima. They're similar in size and texture to great northerns and are interchangeable with them. Although you may not find them in all grocery stores, they're generally sold everywhere in the country.

Navy Beans, Pea Beans, Small White Beans. Although we have three names, they seem to represent only two bean varieties. Commercial labeling on them is confusing. Navy beans, which are grown mainly in Michigan, are smaller than great northerns, but larger than the small whites grown in California. "Pea beans" sometimes refers to navy beans and sometimes means a small white bean (though not necessarily grown in California). To confuse matters more, some packages are marked, "Navy Pea Beans." Don't worry too much about the names. These beans are pretty much interchangeable, although the small white (or pea) bean is smaller and firmer than the standard navy beans. These beans are available, under one name or another, everywhere. Usually they are the cheapest of the white beans.

Pink and Red Beans

Red Kidney Beans. Of all the kidney beans, these are the darkest, being deep red when dried and turning almost purple-black when cooked. They are often used in chili and are grown from coast to coast. They do well in the home garden and are a good choice for drying yourself.

Light Red Kidney Beans. Another popular choice for chili, these look just like dark red kidney beans except for being lighter in color. When cooked they look like pintos and pinks, a rosy brown. They're available from coast to coast, although some grocery stores carry only red or light red, not both. They can substitute for dark red kidney beans.

Cranberry Beans. Sometimes called "shellouts," cranberry beans are a mottled pink and beige bean, a little smaller than kidney beans, typically found in the East and practically impossible to find on the West Coast.

Pinto Beans. These are common in the West and Southwest and look like cranberry beans except they are pale pink spotted with brown.

Pink Beans. Pinks look like pintos without the spots. Pinks, pintos, and cranberry beans are interchangeable. You never know where you will find pink beans. They seem to be available all over the country, but not in all grocery stores.

Small Red Beans. These beans are a bright red, sometimes called a red pea bean and sometimes called "Mexican chili bean." They are smaller, firmer, and less mealy than kidney beans. Common in the West and Southwest, they are hard to find in some parts of the East, but when you can find them, they make a nice change from kidney beans and give a completely different character to chili. When you can't get them, any of the other pink or red beans may be substituted, although the results will be somewhat different.

Peas

Black-Eyed Peas, Yellow-Eyed Peas. Both of these are oval, with a black or yellow spot in the curve. They are actually beans, but are always called "peas" in the south where they are traditional. They cook faster than most dried beans and have a smooth, rather than mealy, texture when cooked. Although you can use black-eyed and

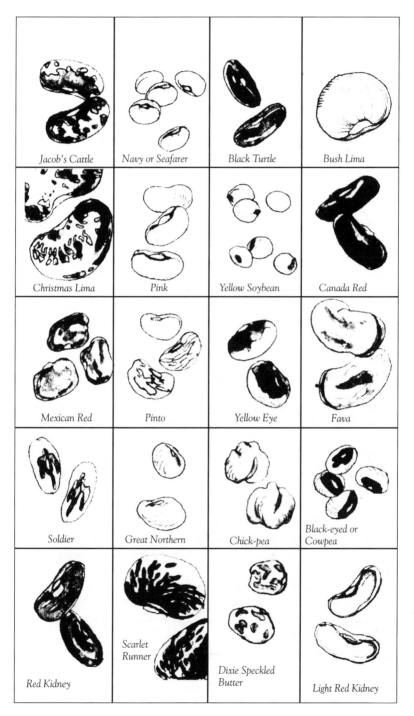

Jacob's Cattle	Navy or Seafarer	Black Turtle	Bush Lima
Christmas Lima	Pink	Yellow Soybean	Canada Red
Mexican Red	Pinto	Yellow Eye	Fava
Soldier	Great Northern	Chick-pea	Black-eyed or Cowpea
Red Kidney	Scarlet Runner	Dixie Speckled Butter	Light Red Kidney

yellow-eyed peas interchangeably, which is good because the yellow variety is hard to find in some places, nothing else substitutes properly for them. But you can find one variety or the other almost everywhere.

Chick-peas, Garbanzos, Ceci Peas, Spanish Peas. Four names apply to one bean. Chick-peas are round but irregular, pale yellow, with wrinkled skins and very firm texture. Small stores often do not carry them (except sometimes canned), but you can find them in virtually all larger supermarkets and natural food stores. No other bean substitutes.

Split Peas. Split peas really are peas and they really are split. You can buy green or yellow, with the yellow ones somewhat less common than the green. The two are similar in taste and can be used interchangeably in any recipe where color is not a factor.

Whole Dried Green Peas. Although not as popular as split peas, whole green peas show up in most grocery stores. They are another good grow-and-dry-it-yourself project. You can begin with garden peas you didn't get to pick when they were young and sweet. Just let them mature until the pods dry, then shell them out.

Beans with Exotic Flavor

Lentils. People have been eating lentils since biblical times. Today they're available almost everywhere. They're a brownish olive-drab color, although some natural food stores carry red lentils which, actually, are orange in color. Both kinds look something like miscolored split peas, except that each whole lentil is about the size of one half of the divided "split" pea. Older recipes recommend long soaking and cooking for lentils. Newer lentil varieties the kind you find in stores today, cook much more quickly than their predecessors and don't have to be soaked at all any more. Red and brown lentils taste somewhat the same, but absolutely nothing else tastes like a lentil — there's no substitute.

Black Beans, Turtle Beans. Black beans have been popular in South America for many years, but because of their musky-spicy taste which blends better with Latin seasonings than those typically North American, black beans have been slow to catch on in the United States. Gourmet cooks consider them the "Cadillac" of beans, but that still limits them to a small corner of the eating populace. There are many varieties of black bean, ranging in size between navy beans and kidney beans. When you nick the skin of a cooked black bean, it is which underneath.

Soybeans. This is the only bean that supplies complete protein without being supplemented by grains or dairy products. It used to be difficult to find soybeans anywhere except in natural foods stores, but these days they're increasingly visible on grocery store shelves. Soybeans are easy to grow in your garden if your season is long enough for them to mature before the frost — they need about 20–30 days more than most snap and wax beans, depending on the variety. No soybean recipes are included in this collection because whole books are devoted to that single versatile bean.

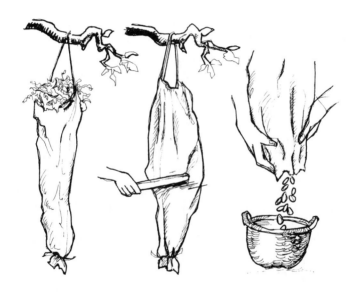

Beans are threshed when the plants and the pods are thoroughly dry. Here's an easy system. Hang a burlap cylinder from a branch. Tie off the bottom opening. Fill the bag with beans and beat with a blunt stick. The beans will fall to the bottom of the bag and can be poured out into a container.

Grow Your Own Beans

The previous list by no means covers al the kinds of dried beans you might encounter. Not only will you find lesser-known varieties limited to small regional pockets, but also you will discover that the home gardener who lets green and yellow snap beans grow to maturity and then dries them will produce beans of every shape and color. One popular oddity, the decorative scarlet runner, planted mainly for its flowers, produces a large, spectacular dried bean splashed with red. It's delicious, but probably available nowhere commercially.

If you want to dry your own beans, the simplest way is to leave some of the beans on the vine until the hulls have dried and begun to open, and then to shell out the beans. However, this method invites insect problems, and you may lose as many beans as you can save. A better method is to pull up the plants and allow them to dry in an airy place. Once the hulls are brittle, you can shell out the beans easily. Then put the shelled beans in the oven on warm for about an hour to kill any insects or larvae.

You'll find that beans you grow and dry yourself often cook faster and are less firm than commercial beans; this is because of differing varieties and because your own beans may be stored a shorter time.

Store beans in a tight container in a cool, dry, dark place. I keep mine in Mason jars in the pantry, rotating older jars to the front when I add newer ones.

Although cookbooks tend to be conservative in their estimates of how long you can keep dry beans (*The Woman's Day Encyclopedia of Cookery* says one year on your kitchen shelf), properly dried and stored beans will keep indefinitely without significant deterioration.

Cooking Information

Here are a few tips for those of you who have never cooked dried beans before.

Washing and Soaking

Always wash beans thoroughly and remove foreign objects and bad beans. You *can* cook beans without soaking them first, but it takes forever and they end up unevenly cooked, with poor texture. For generations the method for soaking beans was to cover them with cold water and let them stand overnight in a cool place. It's still a good method.

The home economists of the California Dry Bean test kitchen prefer a variation on the old method, worked out by the USDA: the overnight salt soak. For each cup of dried beans, add 3 cups of cold water and 1 teaspoon salt. Allow to stand overnight, as with the old method. Testers say the salt in the water helps the beans absorb moisture more evenly, which results in better shape and more even cooking. However, if you are trying to reduce the amount of salt in your diet, you would want to avoid this method.

The Quick-Soak Method. The quick-soak is good when you haven't planned ahead to soak beans overnight. Put the beans in a large pot, cover them with water, bring to a boil, and cook for 2 minutes with a lid on the pan. Then remove the pan from the heat and let the beans stand, covered, for 1 or 2 hours. This is equivalent to as much as 15 hours of plain soaking.

Simmering

No matter how you soak the beans and no matter what recipe you plan to use, the next step is to simmer the beans until they are tender. In past years, nutritionists urged cooks to simmer the beans in their soaking water. Today no one's quite sure. Nutritionists have determined that the loss of nutrients in discarded soaking water is minimal, and some cooks feel that cooking in fresh water makes the beans taste better and also helps cut down on what Julia Child calls the "root-ti-toot-toot" problem. However, any digestive problems you have with beans settle down as you eat them more regularly and your body becomes accustomed to the B vitamins and extra fiber provided by beans. And most people wouldn't be able to tell by taste whether beans had been cooked in fresh water or soaking water. So, ultimately, it doesn't seem to matter much one way or the other. I still follow the old cooks' advice of cooking in the soaking water when it tastes sweet and replacing it with fresh when the soaking water tastes bitter. It is important to remember that if you use the salt soak, you should cook in fresh water or you will end up with oversalted beans.

One old-time simmering trick you should avoid is putting baking soda in the cooking water to speed up cooking. Don't do it; it destroys vitamins in the beans.

If you have trouble with beans foaming as you cook them, you can add a tablespoon of oil or butter to the cooking water, or you can tilt the pan lid and lower the heat until the foaming subsides.

The simmering time to make beans tender varies considerably depending on the variety of bean, how long it's been stored and how dry it is. If time matters at all, add tomatoes, vinegar, or wine toward the end of the simmering, otherwise the acid will slow the cooking.

When you're planning, it's best to allow a little extra time for beans, just in case they take longer than the recipe suggests. You'll know they're done when the skins begin to break open and a bean is tender all the way through when you bite into it.

Keeping It Simple

All this discussion of how to cook beans, combined with the comparatively long cooking times of most of the recipes, could make you feel that cooking beans is a complicated, time-consuming process. It is not. Indeed, there's not much you can do to spoil a bean — it tolerates overcooking, fluctuating temperatures, and even interrupted cooking. As for time, beans do take a lot of it, but it's not *your* time. You don't have to watch or stir them through most of the cooking, and if you use low heat and proper utensils, you don't even have to be in the house for most of it.

The only thing that seems crucial in cooking beans well is long, slow cooking at low, low temperatures, rather than shorter cooking at high temperatures. The beans develop their own flavor; their skins are less inclined to fall off; and when the skins to come off, they gradually disintegrate into the bean broth.

Timetable for Cooking Beans

	Soaked beans cooked tender regular method	Soaked Beans cooked tender pressure cooker	Unsoaked beans cooked tender pressure cooker
Baby limas and butter beans	30 to 60 minutes	not recommended	not recommended
Great northern and marrow beans	2½ to 3 hours	8 minutes	20 minutes
Navy, pea, and small white beans	3 to 3½ hours	10 minutes	30 to 35 minutes
Kidney, pink, cranberry, and pinto beans	2 to 2½ hours	5 to 7 minutes	20 to 25 minutes
Small red beans	3 to 3½ hours	10 minutes	30 to 35 minutes
Black-eyed peas	30 to 50 minutes	not recommended	not recommended
Chick-peas	4 hours	15 to 20 minutes	45 minutes
Split peas*	40 to 60 minutes	not recommended	not recommended
Whole dried green peas	60 to 70 minutes	not recommended	not recommended
Lentils*	30 to 40 minutes	not recommended	not recommended
Black beans	2½ hours	8 to 10 minutes	25 to 30 minutes

Soaking may be eliminated; cooking time then approximately doubles.

All cooking times here are the minimum; longer cooking times may be necessary depending on the dryness of the bean. Hard water also lengthens cooking times.

Special Cases

The value of slow cooking might lead you to believe a slow crockery cooker should be ideal for cooking beans. I haven't found this to be so. It is possible to cook beans in a crockery cooker. You must follow the manufacturer's directions for heat settings and you must be prepared to wait longer than usual for the beans to get done. I have a lentil recipe, for example, which requires cooking the lentils overnight with baking soda, then mixing them with other ingredients and cooking them up to 10 hours more. Normally, lentils cook faster than most beans and require no soaking. In other slow cooker recipes for beans you must cook the beans on the stove before putting them into the cooker. Somehow it doesn't seem worth the trouble. And, despite all this long procedure, the good slow-simmered bean flavor doesn't develop. My theory is that it has something to do with how little evaporation takes place in crockery slow cooking.

On the other hand, a well-seasoned cast-iron Dutch oven, barely simmering on the back of an old woodstove or in your oven can produce memorable beans. Cast iron distributes the heat evenly and holds it steady; beans like that. If you don't have a woodburning stove, setting the Dutch oven in your oven with the heat at about 200°F gives much the same results. Be sure your kettle is well-seasoned before you try to cook beans in it. A poorly seasoned Dutch oven will release an iron flavor into the beans, making them taste like rusty nails, and may also turn them gray. (To be sure your Dutch oven is adequately seasoned, rub it heavily with lard or other fat and heat it in a warm oven for several hours. Wipe the dutch oven clean with dry cloths or paper towels. Avoid washing it with detergents.)

Pressure Cooking

However desirable it may be to cook beans slowly, sometimes you need them in a hurry. You can cook them quickly in a pressure cooker, if you're *careful*. An entire generation of us grew up with mothers who were forever telling tales about vegetable soup on the ceiling. Because beans tend to foam and can clog the vent in a pressure cooker, you need to take special precautions to keep your beans off the ceiling.

You need not soak beans for pressure cooking, just wash them and put them into the cooker with about 3 or 4 cups of water for each cup of beans. Bring the beans to a boil, put on the lid of the pressure cooker according to the manufacturer's instructions, and set the gauge at 15 pounds. Use the cooking times listed on page 11 to figure out the proper cooking time. Keep the heat adjusted so that the jiggle of the pressure gauge is steady but not frantically fast. At the end of the cooking time, hold the pressure cooker under cold running water to reduce the pressure. Vent any remaining steam and open the pressure cooker according to the directions for your particular pressure cooker.

For safety, you should never fill your pressure cooker much more than one-third full when cooking beans. A little fat added to the cooking water will help keep foam down, but lima beans foam too much to be successful in the pressure cooker; split peas and black-eyed peas can be risky, too. For chick-peas, however, the pressure cooker is a great gift because they take so long to soften with ordinary cooking methods.

Recipes

Many of the recipes in this collection do not call for meat; many of the recipes which do can be made without it. If you want to omit meat from any recipe, simply proceed without it, using vegetable stock rather than meat or chicken stock wherever stock is an ingredient. Since meat adds its own flavor to beans, if you omit it, you may want to add some extra flavoring agent — a little extra butter or olive oil, a clove of garlic, a carrot, or extra herbs, for instance. The few recipes where the meat is essential have been noted so that you can skip them entirely. If you are avoiding meat for economic rather than health or philosophic reasons, you will find these recipes taste as good if you use less than the amount of meat specified, especially if you are sure to use a well-flavored stock as part of the cooking liquid.

On the other hand, if you want to add a little meat to any of the meatless recipes, you can do that, too. Simply put it in with the beans anytime after the soaking step. If you want to add sausage or any fatty meat, it's a good idea to brown it and drain away the fat first. And if you have scraps of leftover meat you don't want to waste, cut them fine and add them to your beans near the end of the cooking time. Small amounts of meat added to beans enhance their protein value in much the way combining beans with dairy products or grains does.

Just Plain Beans

Don't miss the pleasure of plain, unadorned, cooked beans from time to time. If you always have your beans seasoned with ham or chili powder or tomatoes, it's easy to tire of them, but a "basic" bean, like a plain potato, is something you can eat over and over, enjoying its good taste each time.

As you eat beans plain — that is, simply soaked and simmered to tenderness — more often, you'll become increasingly familiar with the flavor subtleties unique to each variety and then, truly, it will be impossible for you to find beans boring. You will find them, along with a glass of milk, an easy and logical breakfast. Sprinkled with grated cheese and raw green onions, served with whole grain bread, plain beans satisfy you thoroughly at lunch. And, at dinner, a bowl of plain beans served like a vegetable complements the flavors of your best recipes and guarantees that nobody will go away still hungry, even if you end up serving several more people than you had anticipated.

But, when just plain beans don't appeal, then it is time to turn to the recipes that follow.

Soups and Stews

MANY BEAN SOUP

This is, without question, the best bean soup I've ever tasted. Even people who don't like beans like this soup.

- ⅓ cup great northern beans
- ⅓ cup dried baby limas
- ⅓ cup lentils
- ⅓ cup pinto beans
- ⅓ cup red beans
- 6 cups water
- ½ teaspoon salt
- 1 medium onion, coarsely chopped
- 1 celery rib with leaves, coarsely chopped
- 2 garlic cloves, minced
- 1 bay leaf
- 2 ham hocks
- ¼ cup salt pork cubes

Soak the beans together overnight or use the quick-soak method. Put the beans in a kettle with 6 cups of the soaking water or use fresh water. Add the salt, onion, celery, garlic, bay leaf, ham hocks and salt pork. Reduce the heat, cover the pan, and simmer until all the beans are tender and some are beginning to fall apart, probably about 3 hours.

Cool the ham hocks so you can remove any meat on them and return the meat to the beans.

Time: 3 hours (after the beans are soaked)

YIELD: 6 SERVINGS

PUREED BEAN SOUP

This is one of my favorite ways to prepare dried beans. It's good for people who dislike the texture of whole beans, and it's soothing and easily digested.

1	cup marrow beans
4	cups water
½	teaspoon salt
1	medium onion, chopped
1	medium carrot, chopped
1	celery rib with leaves, chopped
1	clove garlic, minced
1	bay leaf
2	tablespoons butter
1	cup chicken broth *or* vegetable stock *or* milk
2	tablespoons chopped parsley
2	tablespoons chopped chives

Soak the beans overnight or use the quick-soak method. Put the beans into a kettle with 4 cups of the soaking water or use fresh water. Add salt. Bring to a boil, lower the heat, cover the pan, and simmer until the beans are very tender, at least 2 hours.

Add the chopped onion, carrot, celery, garlic, and bay leaf. Cook about 30 minutes longer, until the vegetables are soft. Remove the bay leaf, and puree the bean mixture in the blender, food processor, or food mill. Stir in the butter and as much stock or milk as you need to thin the soup to a consistency you like. Return the soup to the heat until it is very hot, but if you thinned it with milk, be careful not to let it boil.

Chilled bean puree soup is a summer gourmet specialty in some French restaurants. To serve the soup chilled, proceed exactly as you would for serving it hot, but instead of returning it to the pan to reheat, cool it further, and refrigerate it at least 6 hours. It tends to thicken as it cools, so you may need to add more milk or stock. Also, test the seasoning, you may want to zip it up a bit more for serving chilled. Garnish with the parsley and chives.

Time: 2½ hours (after the beans are soaked) for hot soup, plus 6 hours chilling time (or overnight) for cold soup

YIELD: 6 TO 8 SERVINGS

SPLIT PEA SOUP

If you've never had split pea soup made any way except with ham, this will be a treat. Ham tends to overpower the delicate flavor of split peas; in this recipe that delicate flavor predominates.

1	pound (about 2¼ cups) green *or* yellow split peas
6	cups chicken *or* vegetable stock
2	tablespoons butter
1	teaspoon salt
1	whole clove
1	medium onion, chopped
1	celery rib with leaves, chopped
1	small clove garlic, minced
1	carrot, chopped
1	small potato, unpeeled and diced
1	cup diced cooked chicken *or* turkey (optional)

Wash and sort the split peas. Put them in a 6-quart kettle with all the other ingredients except the chicken or turkey. Bring to a boil. Lower the heat, cover the pot, and simmer, stirring occasionally to keep the peas from sticking to the bottom of the pan, for 2 to 3 hours. The peas and vegetables should be very soft and begin to fall apart. The thicker part of the soup will tend to sink to the bottom of the pan and should be stirred up before serving, or you can puree the soup before serving. Stir in the chicken or turkey, just about 5 minutes before serving. Parmesan cheese makes a good garnish.

Time: 2 to 3 hours (if peas are soaked first; preparation time after soaking is 30 to 40 minutes)

YIELD: 6 TO 8 SERVINGS

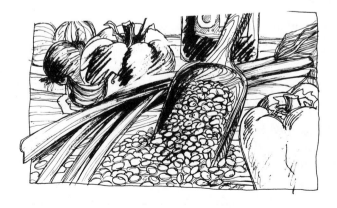

BLACK BEAN SOUP

The flavor of black beans is more spicy than that of most beans, and to some the grayish/black color of the cooked beans and broth is downright unappealing. But to trained taste buds, black bean soup is a treat; no gourmet cookbook would be without a recipe.

1	cup dried black beans
4	cups water
½	teaspoon salt
1	celery rib with leaves, chopped
1	medium onion, chopped
1	leek, white part only, chopped
2	ham hocks
1	bay leaf
½	teaspoon dried thyme
2	tablespoons dry sherry
2	hard-cooked eggs

Soak the beans overnight or use the quick-soak method. Drain the beans and put them into a kettle with 2 cups of fresh water. Add all the remaining ingredients, except the eggs and sherry. Bring to a boil, lower the heat, cover the pan, and simmer until the beans are tender and the meat is falling off the ham hocks, about 3 hours.

Remove the ham hocks and set aside to cool. Scoop out about ½ cup of the cooked beans and puree the rest in a blender, food processor, or food mill. Return the puree to the pan, add the reserved beans and all the bits of meat you can pick off the ham bones. If the soup seems too thick, thin it with a little hot water or stock. Bring almost to a boil, then stir in the sherry. Serve garnished with thin slices of hard-cooked egg.

Time: 3 hours (after the beans are soaked)

YIELD: 6 SERVINGS

Weights and Measures of Beans

1 cup dried beans = 2 to 3 cups cooked beans
1 pound dried beans = 2¼ to 2⅓ cups dried beans
1 pound dried beans = 6 to 7 cups cooked beans

MINESTRONE

You can use any dried beans, or even a combination, to make mine-strone. I prefer small white beans because they hold their shape.

¾ cup dried *or* 2 cups cooked beans with some of the liquid
3 cups water (if you use uncooked beans)
½ teaspoon salt (if you use uncooked beans)
2 tablespoons chopped parsley
1 leak, white part only, chopped
1 medium onion, chopped
2 celery ribs with leaves, chopped
2 garlic cloves, minced
3 tablespoons olive oil
6 cups water *or* stock
2 cups chopped fresh *or* canned tomatoes
2 cups mixed raw vegetables, chopped
1 cup raw macaroni
salt and pepper to taste
oregano *or* basil (optional)

If you are using uncooked beans, soak them overnight or use the quick-cook method. Put them in a kettle with 3 cups of the soaking water or use fresh water. Add salt. Bring to a boil, lower the heat, cover the pan, and simmer until the beans are tender, about 2½ hours.

Put the chopped parsley, leek, onion, celery, and garlic together on a cutting board and chop everything together until all the ingredients are minced fine, almost to a paste. Heat the olive oil in the bottom of the soup kettle, and sauté the chopped ingredients in it until they begin to soften. Add the water or stock and the tomatoes and bring everything to a boil. Add the coarsely chopped vegetables, raw macaroni, and cooked beans with liquid. Simmer everything together about 20 minutes, or until vegetables and macaroni are tender. Season to taste with salt, pepper, and oregano or basil.

Time: 20 to 30 minutes (after beans are cooked); for uncooked beans, 3 hours (after beans are soaked)

YIELD: 8 TO 10 SERVINGS

It's Easy to Sprout Beans

Wash 1 cup of dried beans and pick out any which are broken. Soak them overnight in warm water. Drain. Place the beans in a glass jar and cover the mouth with a screen or cheesecloth and keep the jar in a warm, dark place for 3 to 5 days. Rinse the beans gently with warm water, draining thoroughly each time, at least 3 times a day, more often if the weather is very warm. Sprouts are ready when they are 1 or 2 inches long. Rinse them thoroughly in cold water, drain well, and store in a covered container in the refrigerator. The sprouts will keep about 4 days. One cup of dried beans yields 4 cups of sprouts.

CASSOULET

Cassoulet sounds French and fancy, but basically it is simply an uncommonly good meat and bean stew. It's one of the few recipes in this collection that just can't be made properly without meat.

2	cups great northern *or* marrow beans
1	cup water
6	cups stock
3	garlic cloves, minced
1	large onion, chopped
2	celery ribs with leaves, chopped
2	tablespoons chopped parsley
1	bay leaf
½	teaspoon dry thyme leaves
½	teaspoon salt
¼	teaspoon pepper
	a bone from a cooked pork roast *or* 3 pork chops, browned
½	cup dry white wine
10	chicken thighs *or* drumsticks *or* wings (*or* a combination)
½	pound smoked sausage

Soak the beans overnight or use the quick-soak method. Drain the beans and put them into a kettle with 1 cup fresh water, the stock, garlic, onion, celery, parsley, and seasonings. Bring to a boil, cover the pan, reduce the heat, and simmer for 1 hour. Then add the pork bone or chops. Continue simmering another 1½ hours or until the beans are tender.

Turn the beans into a large baking dish. Cut the pork into small pieces and add it to the beans. Pour on the wine. Arrange the chicken pieces on top of the beans, cover the casserole, and bake in a 200°F oven for about 6 hours. Check the beans occasionally to be sure they have lots of liquid. If they appear to be drying out, add stock. Cassoulet should be almost soupy, not as thick as ordinary baked beans.

While the beans are baking, cut the sausage into small pieces and brown it in the skillet. Drain off as much fat as possible. About 30 minutes before you want to serve the cassoulet, stir in the sausage, raise the oven heat to 350°F and bake about 30 minutes with the cover removed to brown the top of the beans and chicken. Be sure to keep adding stock, if necessary, to keep the beans juicy. (You can omit the browning step if you're busy. It's mainly for appearance's sake. If you do, just stir in the sausage and finish baking at the lower temperature in a covered casserole.)

Baking time for cassoulet is flexible. Shorten it to as little as 2 hours or extend it to 8 hours or more. Raise or lower the oven heat accordingly. Long, slow cooking gives superior flavor.

Time: 4½ to 10½ hours (after beans are soaked); may be started a day ahead

YIELD: 10 SERVINGS

LOUISIANA RED BEANS AND RICE

Red beans and rice have long been the classic "poor man's food." The combination is a perfect example of old folkways producing intuitively what we know now, scientifically, to be a perfect complementary protein combination. But it would be a pity to make red beans and rice sound like a nutritional medicine and lose the gourmets' interest, for this may be the best recipe in this collection. I've never served it to anybody who didn't enjoy it.

2⅓	cups (1 pound) red kidney beans
3	cups water
½	teaspoon salt
2 or 3	ham hocks
1	medium onion, chopped
1	garlic clove, minced
1	celery rib with leaves, chopped
1	bay leaf
1	pound sausage
2	cups cooked brown rice
	chopped green onion
	grated cheddar cheese

Soak the beans overnight or use the quick-soak method. Drain and put them in a kettle with 3 cups fresh water. Bring to a boil, reduce the heat, cover the pan, and simmer for about 30 minutes. Add the salt, ham hocks, onion, garlic, celery, and bay leaf. Simmer 2 hours or longer. Add water if the mixture gets too thick. The beans will be tender in 2 hours, but longer simmering makes the flavor richer.

About 30 minutes before serving, remove the ham hocks, and cool them until you can remove the meat from the bones. Cut the meat into small pieces and return it to the kettle. Meanwhile, cut the sausage into small pieces and fry until brown. Drain away the fat and stir the sausage into the beans. Simmer over very low heat to blend the flavors.

To serve, spoon the beans over the rice on a large platter and garnish with generous amounts of chopped green onion and grated cheddar cheese.

Time: 2½ hours minimum (after beans are soaked)

YIELD: 8 TO 10 SERVINGS

LENTIL-RICE STEW

¼   **cup olive oil**
1   **large onion, sliced**
½   **cup raw long-grain brown rice**
2   **cups lentils**
½   **teaspoon salt**
6   **cups water**
1   **cup canned tomatoes**
6   **cups coarsely chopped raw chard**
coarsely ground black pepper
vinegar
yogurt *or* **sour cream**

Heat the olive oil in the bottom of a heavy saucepan or Dutch oven. Sauté the onion and rice in the oil over medium high heat until the onions are golden and the rice grains are coated with oil and look translucent. Add the lentils, salt, and water. Bring to a boil, reduce the heat, cover the pan, and simmer until the rice is done, about 45 minutes. By then the lentils should be tender too; if not, simmer about 20 minutes longer. Add water if the mixture becomes too thick.

When everything is tender, add the tomatoes and cook 10 minutes longer. About 5 minutes before serving, stir in the chopped chard and steam with the lid on just until the greens are wilted. Season with the pepper and vinegar, top with yogurt or sour cream.

Time: 1¼ hours

YIELD: 8 SERVINGS

KIDNEY BEAN STEW WITH SPOONBREAD

Red kidney beans are best for this because they make a rich gravy. The chocolate sounds wrong but don't omit it. You won't taste the chocolate, and it does add depth of flavor to this meatless stew. Incidentally, the combination of milk, eggs, and corn in the spoonbread plus the protein of the beans make this a super high-protein meal.

2⅓	cups (1 pound) red kidney beans
6	cups water
1	teaspoon salt
1	medium onion, chopped
1	green pepper, chopped
1	clove garlic, minced
1	cup tomato sauce
2	teaspoons chili powder
1	dried hot red pepper (optional)
1	tablespoon grated unsweetened chocolate

Soak the beans overnight or use the quick-soak method. Put them into a kettle with 6 cups of the soaking water or use fresh water. Add salt. Bring to a boil, cover the pan, lower the heat, and simmer for 1 hour. Add the remaining ingredients and simmer, uncovered, about 1½ hours longer, or until the beans are tender but not falling apart, and the liquid has thickened into a rich gravy. Keep the heat low during this simmering and stir the beans from time to time so they don't stick to the bottom of the pan, which is more likely to happen when you simmer them uncovered.

Be sure to remove the hot red pepper before serving. To serve, ladle each helping over a generous portion of hot spoonbread.

Time: 2½ hours (after beans are soaked)

YIELD: 6 SERVINGS

SPOONBREAD

3   cups cold milk
1   cup cornmeal
3   eggs
2   tablespoons butter, melted
1   teaspoon salt
3   teaspoons baking powder

Mix together 2 cups of the cold milk and the cornmeal in a saucepan. Bring to a low simmer and cook, stirring often, until the milk is absorbed and the mixture is thick. Cool. Meanwhile, separate the eggs and mix the yolks together with the remaining milk, melted butter, salt, and baking powder. Whip the egg whites until stiff, as for making a soufflé. Gradually stir the liquids into the cornmeal mixture, taking care to mash out any lumps. Then fold the cornmeal mixture into the beaten egg whites. Pour the batter into an ungreased 8-cup baking dish. Bake at 350°F for 40 to 45 minutes. Do not overbake. Spoonbread should be slightly moist in the center when you serve it.

Time: 1 hour

YIELD: 6 SERVINGS

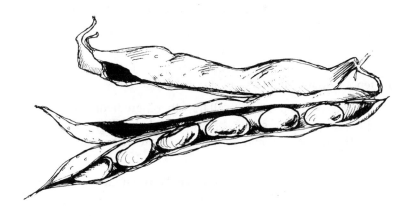

Other Main Dishes

BEAN-RICE SQUARES

You can use any beans, but pinks make a nice color contrast. This recipe is from the Idaho Bean Commission. It's excellent.

¾	cup dried beans (or 2 cups cooked beans)
3	cups water (for cooking dried beans)
1	egg, beaten
1	cup milk
½	teaspoon salt
1	teaspoon Worcestershire sauce
½	teaspoon dry mustard
¼	cup chopped green onion
1	cup cooked brown rice
1½	cups grated cheese: Swiss, cheddar, *or* a combination

Soak the beans overnight or use the quick-soak method. Put the beans in a kettle with 3 cups of the soaking water or fresh water. Bring to a boil, lower the heat, cover the pan, and simmer until the beans are tender, about 2 hours. Cool slightly and drain.

Mix the cooked beans with all the other ingredients and pour into a well-greased 8 inch square baking pan. Bake 40 to 45 minutes at 325°F. The mixture should be just set, like a custard, but not dried out.

Time: 40 minutes (after beans are cooked); 2 hours and 45 minutes for uncooked beans (after the beans are soaked)

YIELD: 4 SERVINGS

ZUCCHINI STUFFED WITH BEANS

4	medium zucchini
½	cup finely chopped onion
2	tablespoons butter
1	cup cottage cheese
1	cup cooked brown rice
1	cup cooked pink *or* red beans
2	beaten eggs
½	teaspoon salt
1	cup grated cheese

Trim the ends of the zucchini and steam the squash in a small amount of boiling water for 8 minutes or until barely tender. Cool. Cut each zucchini in half lengthwise, scoop out the centers, discarding any large seeds and dice the rest of the centers.

While the zucchini is steaming and cooling, sauté the onion in the butter until tender. Combine this mixture with the cottage cheese, rice, beans, eggs, salt, and chopped zucchini centers. Spoon the mixture into the hollowed out zucchini shells. Arrange the shells in a long, shallow pan or on a cookie sheet.

Cover loosely with aluminum foil. Bake in a 350°F oven for 25 minutes. Remove the soil, sprinkle the grated cheese on the zucchini, and bake uncovered about 5 minutes more, just until the cheese has melted.

Time: 50 minutes (after beans and rice are cooked)

YIELD: 8 SERVINGS

FRIJOLES REFRITOS (REFRIED BEANS)

Frijoles refritos actually translates more accurately to "reheated beans," since they are fried only once, but "refried" is the usual terminology. Refried beans are basic in Mexican cooking. They appear as a main ingredient in many concoctions, including tacos, and as a side dish with almost everything else.

One Mexican cookbook claims lard in huge quantities is the key to good refried beans and while a small amount of it does add a nice taste, your cardiologist will be relieved to know you can make splendid refried beans with a minimum of fat.

| 3 | cups cooked pinto, pink, *or* kidney beans with cooking liquid |
| 3 to 4 | tablespoons butter, oil, *or* lard |

In a large iron skillet, heat enough fat to cover the bottom of the skillet. Then put in about 1 cup of cooked beans and, with the heat on medium, begin mashing and cooking the beans. As they turn to a paste, continue mashing in more beans, about ½ cupful at a time. From time to time work in ¼ cup of the bean liquid to keep the mixture soft. If the beans stick to the bottom of the skillet, lower the heat slightly and add a little more fat. When all the beans have been mashed in, except for a few you leave whole or in pieces for texture, add a little more liquid and turn the heat very low. Allow the mixture to simmer for about 20 minutes — possibly less — until the bean liquid has been reduced and is part of the bean puree. A slight crust will form around the edges and on the bottom of the pan. When you reach this point, the beans are ready to serve.

Stir in some seasoning such as chili powder, salt and pepper, hot pepper relish, or raw chopped onion, or use the beans in their milder, less-seasoned state.

Time: about 35 minutes (after beans are cooked)

YIELD: 3 CUPS, OR 4 TO 6 SERVINGS

Side Dishes

BOSTON BAKED BEANS

Here's standard baked bean recipe in the New England tradition. You'll note the absence of tomato or catsup. That's because the colonists did not eat tomatoes and, in fact, thought they were poisonous until after 1800.

2	cups small white beans
6	cups water
½	teaspoon salt
¾	cup salt pork cubes
¼	cup brown sugar
¼	cup molasses
½	teaspoon dry mustard

Soak the beans overnight or use the quick-soak method. Put the beans in a kettle with 6 cups of the soaking water or fresh water. Add the salt. Bring to a boil, lower the heat, cover the pan, and simmer the beans until tender, about 2 hours.

Mix the beans and all the cooking water in a baking dish with the salt pork, sugar, molasses, and dry mustard. Cover the casserole and bake the beans at 225°F for 6 to 8 hours or longer. Check occasionally to see if you need to add more water. You may raise the heat and shorten the baking time, but the long, slow cooking produces tastier beans.

Time: 8 to 10 hours (after beans are soaked)

YIELD: 8 TO 10 SERVINGS

FRIED CHICK-PEAS WITH GARLIC

Chick-peas are indestructible; it's almost impossible to cook them too long. When you prepare chick-peas for cooking, wash them extra carefully because the dust and sand sometimes imbedded in the wrinkles of their skin cling tenaciously.

1	cup dried chick-peas
3	cups water
½	teaspoon salt
3	tablespoons olive oil
1	clove garlic
	lemon juice
	black pepper

After a thorough washing, soak the beans overnight or use the quick-soak method. Drain the soaking water. Put the beans into a kettle with 3 cups fresh water. Add the salt. Bring to a boil, reduce the heat, cover the pan, and simmer until the chick-peas are tender, about 4 hours. Check occasionally to be sure the beans are still covered with water and add more water as needed. When the beans are tender all the way through (bite into one to test), drain and cool them.

Heat the oil in a heavy skillet and swirl the garlic around in it a few seconds before adding the beans. Keep the heat medium high and stir the chick-peas around in the skillet gently for about 10 minutes, or until they form a crispy, brown crust on the outside. Put the chick-peas into a serving dish, remove the garlic, and season with lemon juice and pepper.

Time: 15 minutes (after chick-peas are cooked)

YIELD: 2 SERVINGS

BUTTER BEANS

I grew up with this dish. I think probably it's Pennsylvania Dutch in origin. Butter beans, warm or cold, make a delicious, if somewhat unorthodox, breakfast. More traditionally, serve them instead of potatoes with any roast meat or fowl.

1	cup large dried limas
3	cups water
½	teaspoon salt
1	tablespoons brown sugar
1	tablespoon butter
1	cup water
¼ to ½	cup cream

Soak the beans overnight or use the quick-soak method. Put the beans into a saucepan with 3 cups of the soaking water or fresh water. Add the salt. Bring to a boil, reduce the heat, and cover the pan. Simmer for about 2 hours, adding water from time to time if necessary, until the beans are tender. Turn the beans and the cooking liquid into a baking dish, mix in the brown sugar and butter, and bake in a 225°F oven, uncovered, for about 6 hours, adding water as needed to keep the beans covered. As the limas cook at the low temperature, the liquid will become thick, like gravy.

Just before serving, remove the beans from the oven and stir in enough cream to thin the gravy to a consistency you like.

Time: 8 hours (after beans are soaked)

YIELD: 6 SERVINGS

HUMMUS

This is pureed chick-peas. It's Middle Eastern and is usually served with Arab or pita bread, but it's good as a spread on whole wheat bread or as ● dip for raw vegetables, too.

2 cup cooked chick-peas
1 clove garlic
¼ cup lemon juice
¼ cup olive oil
cold water
2 tablespoons chopped fresh parsley

Puree the chick-peas and garlic in a food processor, blender, or food mill. Mix in the lemon juice and olive oil. Add a little water, if needed, to make a soft mixture. Sprinkle the chopped parsley on top and chill at least 1 hour before serving.

Time: 1 hour and 10 minutes (after the chick-peas are cooked)

YIELD: 6 TO 8 SERVINGS

Seasoning Beans

Herbs and spices vary the taste of beans wonderfully. Some flavors just seem to be made for certain beans. Try these combinations.

- *Cumin* with black beans for an exotic Latin taste.
- *Chili powder* and *paprika* with any red beans or kidney beans or pintos for Mex-Tex flavor.
- *Thyme* with white beans for French overtones.
- *Oregano* and *basil* with white beans for Italian influence.
- *Lemon* and *garlic* with chick-peas for Middle Eastern taste.
- *Molasses* or *brown sugar* with white beans for German flavor.
- *Caraway* and white beans for European suggestions.
- *Curry, cinnamon,* and *clove* with black or white beans for spicy Middle Eastern flavor.